To Cath

WHAT SHE SAID AND WHAT SHE DID

Enjoy!

WHAT SHE SAID AND WHAT SHE DID

DYMPHNA CALLERY

HEADLAND

First published in 1997
by
HEADLAND PUBLICATIONS
38 York Avenue, West Kirby,
Wirral, Merseyside. L48 3JF

Copyright © Dymphna Callery 1997

British Library Cataloguing in Publication Data.
A full CIP record for this book is available from the British Library.

ISBN: 1 902096 00 2

*All rights reserved. No part of this publication may be
reproduced, stored in a retrieval system, or transmitted in
any form, or by any means, electronic, mechanical,
photocopying, recording or otherwise, without the prior
written permission of the publisher.*

*Requests to publish work from this book
must be sent to Headland Publications.*

*Dymphna Callery has asserted her right under Section 77 of
the Copyright, Designs and Patents Act 1988 to be identified
as the author of this book.*

HEADLAND acknowledges the financial
assistance of North West Arts Board

Printed in Great Britain by
L. Cocker & Co., Berry Street, Liverpool.

For Joan and Alastair, with love.

Acknowledgements

Some of these poems have been performed in Liverpool venues, eg The Unity Theatre, Kelechi's, The Bluecoat and on BBC Radio Merseyside. Some have appeared in anthologies published by Poetry Now, and others have appeared in the following magazines: Writing Women, Envoi.

The Pear Tree was first performed at The Unity Theatre in 1994 and then read on BBC Radio Merseyside in 1996 by Kate Brennan.

Cinderella was commissioned by The Unity Theatre and performed there in 1995 by Jane Rogers.

CONTENTS

Counting Coal-Sacks

We are counting coal-sacks:
marking in bar gates each journey
of the men with turned-backed caps
who plod heavily up the drive
and down the garden.

Suspicion never enters our heads:
we think perhaps these dusky men
might forget how many times
they have travelled from cart
to bunker.

They are wise,
and wink their sparkling eyes
under black-furrowed brows
as they pass the kitchen door

where we stand, sanitised
in gingham, our brows creased
with lust and counting.

Sisters

Our world was ringed by cod-liver oil,
hot-water bottles, Izal
boxed in porcelain on a white-tiled wall.

Rules were plain
and followed to the letter:
please and thankyou, saying grace,
turning off the light-switch in the hall.

We grew like bonsai:
hopes so circumscribed
even our dreams were small.

No Legends

My roots bear no legends:
there's no permanence in pavements
chalked with hopscotch,
brick-walls where beads were swapped,
loose cinder tracks we drove
our trolleys down.

On our back-lawns
tents were built from blankets —
castles for princesses to court
the potency of princes;
no nurses and no doctors,
no knights, no white horses.

Under these woollen shrouds
the government of girls endured —
rituals of spite
making boys drink our wee
from old bottles
(really filled with lime-juice
but we never told).

Such never-telling secrets
are stories we still hold
that never will be legends
and never will be sold for money —
but chalked and swapped
and driven across pillows.

Don't Tell Daddy

(i)

The motto we live by in our house
is "don't tell daddy",
observed in whispers
or a glance across the custard,
a nudging knee under the table.

There he sits, back to the window,
conducting the family rites:
bread before cake is the usual sermon,
delivered in dulcet tones
(for Irish churching
breeds an easy lyricism).

We chant his prayers
and we thank his god
(though under our breath
we rattle like snakes),
we know
he values worship more than honesty —

but please
don't tell him I said so.

(ii)

do and be and do and be and do and
do-be do be a good girl and help your
mummy in the .. do and be and do
be a good girl and don't stay out too...
do and be and do and be and do and
do .. **do** make sure your tits are hidden
behind a .. be and Ra-ra-ra-ra and .. **do**
try and be a good girl for your..
doo-be doo-be doo-be doo-be doo...

do all little girls get sick and tired
of **be** like this and **do** like that and do do
do be a good girl now and go to be...
be be be **behave!** and just lay down and
go to sleep —

or do I have to go and tell Daddy ?

(iii)

Your curly head is lodged between my thighs
when I whisper *not yet, please, not now* —
did you hear a creaking on the stairs?

At 2 a.m., aged seventeen, I should be
tucked in bed, not naked here with you.

Shame stains my cheeks at you and me
sprawled across the living room floor;
stale wine and guilt sour my mouth
as Daddy's kettle boils beyond the door.

If I breathe now, what forfeit will I pay ?

(iv)

It was quite a shock at university
to discover that my dad's just like
King Lear. An even greater shock to find
personal analogies are not legitimate in criticism,
for Profs. and Tutors had their catechism
which stated this was not allowed:
Why should we, they asked, *examine women
and their lives?*

Two useful things I learnt from these wise men:
I learnt a sonnet must have fourteen lines,
I also gathered genius breaks the rules.

(v)

You always were, her mother said, *very
sexual;* the word slowly sliding
from her tongue, as though she were tasting
it for the first time. Then she spoke
of her at seventeen, when local boys
hung on the gate and phoned up constantly:
They still rang for you years after you left.
She bit her lip and looked down at her cup:
I used to say you were married.

She poured herself another cup of tea
and said *For god's sake don't tell Daddy.*

Mount Vernon Hospital

You set off in the morning
with a plastic bag
containing your pyjamas,
a book you will not read,
a deck of cards.

You play four-handed bridge:
East, West and South lie dormant
on the laundered bed
as North bids into silence.

The dealer's hands are drenched in sweat:
you wipe them on the sheet
one at a time
and lay the suites in line.

The ace of clubs turns upwards,
East bids four hearts,
West goes cold on spades
and South sits quiet on the king.

Your watch ticks in the quiet.
Nurse says: *it's almost time.*

You lay the queen of clubs
knowing
that when you've won this game
she will pack your pyjamas,
the book you did not read,
this pack of cards
(along with your watch)
back into that plastic bag.

Paddy Reilly

I met a man who looks like you
last Saturday afternoon in the pub.
He knows the town where you were born.

He sang that song you used to sing :
"Come back Paddy Reilly to Ballyjamesduff,
Come back Paddy Reilly to me."

We caught a bus to Bally'duff
the first time you took me home
to peat and thatch, to Mary's soda-bread,
milk stinging into her grey pail.

I met a man who looks like you;
He sang in a deep brown voice:
"Come back Paddy Reilly to me."

I wanted to change Paddy's name to yours.

Visiting The Magi

Give me this planet unburdened,
find me images of gold
gems to lay in my palm
stories worth more than silver,
singing of sun-drenched forests,
love, and the redness of wine.

Give to me only this
and out of the desert
I will travel you to lands
with more than frankinscence and myrrh.

Visiting the magi
I scent more than spices —

I taste the language of stars.

God's Child

pot in a pan
and pan in a pot
who is god's child
who is not

stir and rub
until it's hot
spread it out
with a silver knife

pot in a pan
and pan in a pot
who is god's child
who is not

i'm not
i'm not god's dog

i am a witch
and this is my cauldron
here's a stick
to stir the blood
mix it to a rolling boil
till it sounds like a crocodile

Mermaids' Song

come unto these yellow sands
and then take hands
curtsey when you have lisped
the wild waves' wish
for mercy's sake
come unto these yellow sands

hold your hands
into bubbling surf
then hang them up to dry
come unto these yellow sands
and then join hands
with us

come unto these yellow sands
where no boats pass
and make your screamings ring
out against the rocks
for mercy's sake
come unto these yellow sands
rinse your voices
in the babbling waves
that rush to us

come unto these yellow sands
and then join tongues
with us

come unto these yellow sands
once more
and join your hands
with us

Earth and Moon

earth in a pram
wheeling through space
round and around we go

moon on a stick
waving madder than mad
up and away we go

The Other Me

I really like the Other me
she's more daring
she's more bold
refusing all the fripperies
of silver, men and gold.

And when I heed the Other me
she trails me
hand in hand
across life's beaches, endlessly
sifting fables from the sand.

Sometimes I lose the Other me
she gives so much
and then
she leaves me waiting, lonely
as night winds on the fen.

Then I hate myself, I feel
so vulnerable
so cold
as though there were no heart to me
and rime within my soul.

That's when I pray the Other me
will fetch us home
together
up on the backs of wave-less seas
and high above the heather.

Just like larks the two of us
will fly so far
so wide
that Time will spread eternity
before our every stride.

The Landscape of Different Living

the landscape of different living
is dry
littered with empty shells
and wizened gourds
of the long-departed

such dryness has no heat
no warm vapours
here there is no wind
no rustling of leaves
no trees

only thirst
irksome, pure thirst
a persistent itch
that bites the tongue

words are grit
grained
individual
separate heaps
that cannot make a cairn
but remain single
small
monuments

there are no voids
no chasms
only clean neat divides
Corinthian and arid
chequering the earth

and the dry soil
crumbles
at each silent step

The Pear Tree

It is raining.
A middle-aged woman digs beneath a tree.

When we got you home I pushed you out under this tree. You never cried out here. Lying in the pram holding your feet in your fists. Talking to the leaves. Such wonderful blossom it has in the spring. Like a bride with fifty veils. And masses of pears in October. Baskets of them stacked in the kitchen, remember. Rivers of sweet runny chutney they made. And you'd suck it off slivers of cheese.

She stops digging and rests on her spade.

Such a lovely garden. Down amongst the nettles all the bluebells in a haze. Our very own wood in the wildness here. You used to call it the wilderness. When they called from next door they used to say — can we play in your wilderness. There were fairies down there you said. We'd watch you from the kitchen window. You and the girls from next door. Hiding behind the holly bush. Fingers on lips. Watching. Waiting. Like little statues.

She digs again.

Took you to Peter Pan at Christmas. Dancing along the street between the two of us. One two three and a-upsadaisy. And we'd run along the pavement with you dangling from our arms.
You clapped so hard for Tinkerbell you had blisters on your palms for days. All red for days they were. For days.

Took those two once. Just the once. They told you there was no such thing as Father Christmas. Their garden was all lawn and borders. I never got on with her. Those two always dressed the same. Even their ribbons and socks. Couldn't tell them apart. Not even from their clothes. Not even she could. Never knew which was which. I'd have dressed them differently.

She gathers a pile of debris and moves it to the compost heap. She looks back towards the house.

Such a lovely house. It needed children. Dada said you were a gift from God. Wanted to call you Precious. I don't believe in god. Not like Dada. I went along to church. Yes. But only because he wanted. I never felt it like he did. But you were a gift.

She begins to dig again more furiously.

You don't think it'll be you that's different.
I mean when you get married.
You assume. Assume you can have babies.
Anyone can. So you think you will.
First it's something to avoid. Then you want it.
Then it doesn't happen. Not to you.
Everyone thinks it's so ordinary,
It isn't though.
Not when it doesn't happen to you.

She digs in harder.

She doesn't know how lucky she is. Twins. And a little boy.
Bloody bindweed.

She hurls a sod of earth woven with bindweed towards the compost heap.

Bluebells there are in May. And crocuses before them, Then the daisies spread out over the grass. And by the wall there's willow-herb and long-stemmed buttercups. Poppies too. There must be poppies. All red and delicate. Like those in the picture on the mantelpiece. You in the garden before your First Communion. Stood by the tree with poppies swaying behind you.

She resumes digging.

We should have taken more photographs. Of you on your own. Or with us. Without those two. Always in tow they were. Even at your communion. Out here in the garden before Mass. There they were hand in hand in their dresses from Debenhams with their coy smiles and their same white missals. Little brides of Christ.
Made your frock from my old wedding dress didn't I. Trimmed your socks with lace from the veil. Irish lace. They're in the black lacquer box. The one Grandad brought back from the war. That's where I keep them. Those little socks and the ribbon you were wearing on the last day.
Blood all matted in your hair and your ribbon. I cut it off. I'd never wash it.

She shakes the rain from her hat.

I wasn't her bones and flesh mother.
I loved her just the same.
More maybe.
I was her rearing mother.
I loved her. I couldn't have given her away.

She puts her hat back on and continues digging.

Different genes. That's all. You'd never know by looks she wasn't ours. Everyone said she had Dada's hair. Thick and black and wavy. Glossy as Black Beauty's mane with a shine like new soldiers' boots. A touch of the tar his Mam used to say. Brushed a hundred strokes a night, just like a princess. But never grew up to be one.

You couldn't dance like me. I tried. Sent you to ballet. And ballroom dancing in Connor Street with Miss Cloherty. Still banging her stick on the floor just like when Dada and I used to go there. That's where our genes were different. Two left feet you had Siobhan. That's what Dada said.

She laughs,

You'd never dance like me but you knew it didn't matter. Dada just laughed. He'd pick you up under your armpits and waltz you round the room. Laughing. And your little legs waving in the air.

She stops momentarily to wipe a hair from her eye.

He was holding her leg. When they dug them out of the rubble. His knuckles were still white round her knee. Trying to pull her to safety. Too late. You could see it in his face. He knew it was too late. And I remembered all those years ago at school when Miss Pearson showed us pictures of Pompeii. Pen drawings of people all bent and screaming. Mouths all open. Agape. That's what Dada and the others looked like.

She digs again.

But not you. No. Not you. You were wide-eyed and smiling. Except your eyes had turned to stone.

It was only the ribbon in your hair made me cry. When they brought you out and I held you. I smiled back at your smile. All that dirt and mud all smeared on your face. Scratches all over your cheek. But that didn't matter. No. It was just the way that crumpled ribbon dribbled down your ear.

She stops.

I howled like a vixen.

She sighs and resumes digging.

The pears will be starting soon. And no-one to taste the chutney.

Epitaph for the Witches

it is the ninth wave
which brings about the drowning

out of sorrow
into cries that wring the throat
and tear the air to shreds

as the many-caved mountain
whips her songs to fury
and pares away imposters in her wake

murmers melt to dust
like skin shed from the bone

bones jangle
bereft of fine-webbed threads
that bind the soul to flesh

and blackened rope hangs foul
on silent necks

*yet still the throb of old blood
is staking out its claim.*

Lunatic Girl

(from a painting by Kokoshka)

I know every cut on my body
whether made by scalpel or razor blade
bread knife or scissors.

I ate every scab
picked them clean
waited for new cells to make me pink
as the ribbon in my hair.

It was a race, sometimes,
between teeth and nature
to be honest
but look at my criss-cross wrists —
aren't they beautiful?
They are maps of my soul.

If I get old — when I'm forty maybe —
I won't have cosmetic surgery
I won't invite him to dig his hands
under the skin of my cheeks
and scour me out.
I won't have implants — no foreign matter
will sully me.

I am pure.
I shall stay so.

Waiting....

Surfaces brimming clean
bright as the bare bulb
hung from the ceiling
wiped clear
of grease stains, meat stains, turmeric,
of the time when, after the pub,
you pinned me by the sink
and blood ran down the door
turning to brown dribbles
indistinguishable
from gravy or old ketchup.

Look at that kitchen
serviced by bleach
wanton
in its whiteness
waiting
for coffee stains, tea stains, the turn
of your key in the lock.

Little Lucy

stone stairs
chipped
rock

high heels
tripped
shock

butchers boy
lifts
frock

fairy feet
silken
sock

long legs
fillet
hock

juicy jewel
milky
lock

gentle giant
grips
cock

silent street
stricken
clock

little lucy
bleeds
a lot

Humpty Dumpty

he jumped me
yes he jumped me
then he rumped me
from behind

he pumped and pumped and pumped me
till I fell apart inside

he humped me
then he thumped me
he thumped me
then he humped me

I broke in many pieces
like a mirror cracked inside

he called me his wild strumpet
and his little bit of crumpet

then he cried out like a trumpet
when he shot his sperm inside

and I slumped upon the carpet
left with barely breath or heart beat

he humped me
yes
he humped me
and after humping me
he dumped me

yes
he dumped me
when he'd humped me

he was a proper humpty dumpty
yes he was

but I was the one
no-one
could put back
together
again

What She Said and What She Did

You're problem is, she said
you're all cock.

She didn't!

But I'm more than
just a fanny, she said.

She never!

Yes she did, she said
I'll wait, she said, I'll wait
for someone with a bit more in their skull.

She never!

Yes she did, she said.

And what did he say?

Bitch, he said.

He didn't!

Yes he did, she said.

And then?

Cunt, he said.

He never!

Yes he did, she said.
Fucking cunt, he said.

He didn't!

Yes he did.

What did she do?

She clocked him one, she said.

She didn't!

Yes she did. She said
he shrivelled like a worm.

He never!

He did an' all, she said , he bloody did.

Doc Martens

The way to maintain street-cred
in matters of equality
is to agree
the modern woman's liberated:
no longer need she walk the streets in dread
of rape, or worse —
no likelihood of murder here,
for whether we're in Persia
or in bed
our world is patently aware
the modern woman's liberated —
that's why I wear
Doc Martens on my feet and in my head.

Exceptionally Well
(apologies to Sylvia Plath)

I like a bit of money
Don't we all
Like splashing out
Retail therapy
Shopping is an art
We do it exceptionally well

I like a good old gas
Don't we all
Like to make my belly ache
Laugh therapy
Giggling is an art
We do it exceptionally well

I like a nice red wine
Don't we all
Like to swill it on the tongue
Booze therapy
Drinking is an art
We do it exceptionally well

I like a quiet night in
Don't we all
Like to play romantic tunes
Soul therapy
Crying is an art
We do it exceptionally well

I like a man with muscle
Don't we all
Like to lick salt from his skin
Sex therapy
Bonking is an art
We do it exceptionally well

Penises are not Photogenic
(Sonnet)

Penises are not photogenic :
even softly contoured, their abilit—
y to stretch in size (however scenic
their surroundings or their capabilit—
y to pleasure) means they remain
distastefully purple. I'd forgotten
how unlike the curving heads of cranes
the penis is, until something rotten
crept into your mind and demanded
that I take a photograph of yours.
Should I be surprised that I pandered
to your wish? I worry, of course
that however liberal I'd like to be
there lurks some gene of puritan in me.

Part-time Dad

On Mondays Dad's a bouncer
his dress shirt clean and crisp —
ironed by Mum, of course.

On Tuesdays Dad's a waiter
a white apron round his waist —
not one of Mum's, of course.

On Wednesdays Dad's a boxing ref.
bow-tie in a perfect twist —
knotted by Mum, of course.

On Thursdays Dad's a drummer
down a jazz-club called *The Place* —
Mum's never been, of course.

On Fridays Dad's a boozer
hob-nobbing with his mates —
Mum's never met them, of course.

On Saturdays Dad's a loser
his horses never win the race —
so Mum always says, of course.

On Sundays Dad plays soccer
for the local hospital trust —
Mum cooks the dinner, of course.

Song of a New Salome

On the outside she's a realist
Feet planted firmly on the ground
On the inside she's a hippy
Blowing answers in the wind

She's a dragon, she's a harpy, she's a shrew
She's the one that we all want
But we're too scared to get to know

She'll play polite madonna
She'll pretend to be your whore
Whilst playing angel in the kitchen
She's drawing devils on the wall

She's a dragon, she's a harpy, she's a shrew
She's the one that we all want
But we're too scared to get to know

She'll smarten up for dinner
in an off-the shoulder dress
Wipe the semen from her mouth
Without complaining of the mess

And just when you think you've tamed her
She'll jump another track
Leaving slices of your memory
Scored by nails across your back

She's a dragon, she's a harpy, she's a shrew
She's the one that we all want
But we're too scared to get to know

Contrary Rap

don't / cover me in kisses
don't / brush up to my thighs

don't / nibble at my nipples
don't / send me wild inside

don't / leave me on the corner
don't / take me to the brink

don't / offer me another
don't / buy me something pink

don't / ring me up tomorrow
don't / stay with me tonight

don't / give me lots of flowers
don't / always pick a fight

just remember now
just remember now
just remember now
don't / forget I'm always right

In the Bathroom at Night...

Memoirs dance on the bathroom wall
and no-way no-chance absolutely not-ness
creeps in circles on the carpet.

This is where we read death
in thick moon-cast shadows.

Leaves blackened
by too much thumbing
wrestle with the outside wind.

Will these walls crumble
with the weight of ghosts
still fleshed, still blood-led?

Or will the still-beating endless endlessness
slide in under the door
to set us free?

Mama of Dada

Dada hadda mama Dada hadda
Dada hadda mama Dada hadda
mama mama Dada hadda mama
Dada hadda

hadda dada a mama a mama
a mama hadda Dada a mama
no no mama no Dada no mama no Dada
no no Dada no hadda no mama

Dada hadda a mama
Dada did did did
Dada hadda mama hadda mama
hadda mama named Gertrude
Stein

A Cubist Lament for the Birds —
on the Day of the Oil Slick Disaster
(homage to Gertrude Stein)

A sky full full of birds. Full as full as full of birds. Birds in the in the sky filling the sky full. The sky filling filling up with birds full in flight are the birds. Flying the sky full of flying birds. A sky full of birds flying.

And the chirrup chirruping of the chirruping birds birds in the trees. In the trees full of chirruping the chatter chatter of chirruping of the chattering birds. Birds chatter chatter chattering the chirruping chattering chatter of birds in the trees in the bare trees.

Trees with no not one not even one leaf no leaves on the trees where the leaves are not. Not any not any leaves not leaves no no leaf only the birds the chirruping chirrup of birds only the birds. In the trees the birds chatter chattering in the bare oh so still so bare yes oh so bare trees.

Still still air between the birds in the trees and the birds still flying the sky. Air still as still as still as still no breath of air in the still air as still as a photograph. And the sky still and grey grey and still as still as birds fill the sky flying.

The not moving air not moving is the air the still air that through this air the birds are flying full to the sky the sky. The sky is the sky is the grey sky of the still unmoving air. And the birds the birds are still flying swooping diving filling the sky full of birds.

Only the chirrup chirrup chirrup chattering chirrup of the only bird only one bird left bare in the trees. Trees with no leaves no not one but only one bird one bird chirruping. Why the one bird is one bird is left one bird chirruping. Where are the others. The other other birds that are not chirruping are not not chattering are they flying. Are they flying away from the bare bare trees that have no not even one leaf. Only the one bird one bird just one bird a big bird at the top of the big tree chirrups.

And the sky the sky is empty now empty. An empty sky emptied of the fullness of birds flying. Nothing no nothing but an empty empty sky empty.

Air on Remembrance Sunday

Going home down this lane
late one August afternoon
before you returned to battle
we danced, I seem to remember,
and you vaulted a surprised gate.

Our voices ran wild across the fields
as if respecting some ancient lore
to be unlicensed, lawless, free,
and our laughter veiled the mellowing grass
as tangibly as mist.

Standing at that gate
this November morning
I breathe in air
sharp with lack.

Death by Water

(in memorium: Virginia Woolf)

Gales howl over the marshes, moving
winter on. There will be thrushes soon;
the lawns are jewelled with crocuses.

The strong brown river sidles past:
you stand, hands deep in your pockets
stroking the stones.

Gurgling, conversational,
the waters race to meet the sea
nine miles, at least, from Lewes
where your swollen shape will surface.

I fear death by water, can't conceive
the strength of purpose needed
to choose stones
heavy enough to weight a body.

Song of Freedom
(with thanks to Sean)

I will meet you at the scene
of sweet rebellion
between the body and wine
where time shifts
where the marriage of true minds
admits treachery.

There, in the ash grove,
the graves of other sins
lie in the sun
oblivious to us,
and whilst guns blaze
in the long shadow of the cathedral,
we dance our dance,
sing of the coming of freedom.

Some quiet afternoon
will bring soldiers, tanks positioned
for entry to the garden
where we, haunted by early
summer bees, will go on kissing
liberty.

Angel Poems

(after Rilke)

(i)

Angel! If you had been there with me
As the new April sun gathered up
The afternoon shadows and flung them
Across the river, you would know
The blueness of it — water and sky
Joined by god's brush and palette.
There is nothing like it, Angel.
Nothing compares with the coming of Spring
In the shadow of your arms.

(ii)

They do not know, Angel, of us.
Not anyone. The honesty is astonishing.
Such truth never inhabited stage
Or screen. And that's the best of it:
The hidden-ness, explicit
In the loving loving-ness of the illicit.
This, my Angel, it just is.

(iii)

Angel! If they knew there was a place
We know. Some tract of green
Where love displays what can
Never be mastered: the bold
Exploits of high-flying hearts,
Towers of pleasure, ladders
Standing where the ground is no more
Leaning just on each other, trembling.

Arabesques

(i)

quick, says the bird, find them
find them:
shrubbery paths wind everly inward
lost in a Pinterland
where guesses and knowing slip hand over hand
where a rainbow loses its end
where the dance is the dance
they stand

(i i)

beneath a mulberry tree in the park,
under sycamores in the garden,
in a forest of moss, in a field's corner flattening the hay,
once by a lake (do you remember?) —
I have felt the curve of your warm back
now bending
like a Crusader's bow
in my now-naked arms

(i i i)

it's the middle finger I use
to tease you out

at midnight,
born into the midst of you
I scent oceans, rock-pools, sand
just visited by the sea

and you arrive
with salt on your lips,
sweat on your skin, singing
of the seventh wave

(i v)

the dance dances on and on the dance dances us on on and
on ever on ever on everly everly on the dance dances is
dancing dancing the only dance the ever only dance in the
dance that dances us the dance the dance that the dancer
dances and the dance the dancer yes the dancer and the
dancer is the dance the dancers are the dance the dance
that dances us ever ever everly dancing oh the dancer and
the dance

(v)

turn me in your arms
turn your armoury of kisses to my flesh
and I will enter your skin
as simply as slipping into water

(v i)

free as sand running
your hands chase my flesh

you are my Neruda
giving me
Spring and the cherry trees

Love's Acts Spotlit
Between City Sheets

security beams sweep
across the bed
arcs of light catch my feet
encircling your head
your mouth searches me out

Love's Acts Moonlit
Beneath Starry Skies

naked in the wild
one late summer's night
the moon sheds mild glances
on his rising haunches
her uplifted breasts

All But an Inch

Some morning, just as day breaks glorious
across the river, making gold and blue
yesterday's grey,
you will say
I gave my all,
but one small inch
I saved
in case of war.

Living with Living Love

living I was living
living in living love
loving is that

and loving had to
do a little killing
a little killing
is the way we are loving

killing a little the being
we love
and loving to be living

living with loving
is hard
is hard to bear
is hard to bear killing
a little the love
the love we bear
living with one who is being
loving

Cave Poem

We were stalagmite and stalactite
reaching out into the dark:

Did you hear the stream delving harsh
into the rock?

In its rush towards eventual light
I broke

And half of me was carried off
and half of me's this awkward stump
left behind
listening to your blind need.

The Morning After

we lie all spent

one reeling night has robbed us

we wanted heaven today,
when tomorrow
might have summoned us to paradise

now we lie, wide-eyed,
staring past the pattern
on the wall

whilst the birds swagger out
to greet the dawn.

Paper Boats

We made boats of paper
sailed them into sunsets
navigated them by stars :

they danced
on night-black waters,
sank
deep as mermaids.

One Day

One day
You'll become a quiet memory,
Lying like an oxbow lake upstream.

Then this river will be mine again.

One day.

Charting Course in a Summer Gale

Gale-bound off Tobemory
we shun the sun,
sink low into the belly of our boat
to chart new courses.

Your back against mine
is hot as the south wind,
coarse as Sicilian wine.

Rocked by ferocious winds
singing through shore-grass,
whipping halyards against their masts,
I am anchored, safe,
girdled by the rippling figures of fjords,
the writhing pen of the mapmaker.

Cinderella and the Round Table

*An empty stage on which a large pumpkin sits.
CINDERELLA enters carrying a turnip lantern,
containing a live frog .
She is dressed in a gown made from kitchen items,
eg J cloths, dusters, brillo pads etc.*

[Sings] In a tiny house / By a tiny stream / Lived a lovely lass / Had a lovely dream / And the dream came true / Quite unexpectedly / Cinderella Cinderella Cinderella Ella Ella by the sea-ee-ee-ee-ee. Cinderella-rella-rella. CinderEhla! Cinderee. *[Varying emphasis until...]* CinderehhhHelluva stupid boring name!

I could change it now of course. I've left. If I'm not going to be Missus Charming anymore I don't need to be called Cinderella. I could revert to Cinderbottom. Or Cucendron. That's my real name - Cucendron. It translates as Cinderbottom. Or Cinderslut. They used to call me that before I got caught up in the Prince Charming business. Cinderbottom was considered too rude. So they changed it. Why didn't they call me Dolores I wonder? Delectable Dolores all simmering and sultry. Or Carmen. Sweet sexy Carmen smelling of passion. *[Sings the tune from Bizet's Carmen and dances round]* But I'd been dealt the goody-two-shoes card. So Cinderella I became. *[Notices pumpkin]*

Here we are then. *[Kisses frog three times]* It all depends on you Morg . On the seventh stroke of midnight... If this works sunshine, we'll make history. There you go. *[Turns off light in lantern]* You can travel nice and dark, Morg. I'm not going anywhere without you now I've found you. Now all we have to do is wait.

Have I done everything? Go to forest. Stand beside pumpkin. Kiss frog. Three times. Wait till midnight. On the seventh stroke... It's so exciting. Guin was right. Morgan le Fey is the real thing. Everything she said was true. I mean I didn't even have to show her my palm or anything. She just knew. You are a victim, she said, a victim of circumstances beyond your control. A victim of someone else's spell, she said. Well more or less. In translation as it were. Oh now I see a victim, a lost child of the sea. Well. And she's right. I am. I suspect there was a spare prince on the shelf and no-one would have him.

I never chose him you see. Just got caught up in the thing. There I was cleaning the grate and thinking about how I fancied a night out because there was this dance going on up the road at the castle and, well, to be honest I fancied the man who came with the invitation. Bit of a hunk he was, nice tight arse, and I was daydreaming, you know how you do, what I wouldn't give for a bite of that.

So I was rubbing away at the grate, and as I rubbed I wished. And whoosh, down the chimney comes this big fairy. And then it all started to happen, you know, this coach appeared with these horses all decked out and footmen up on the front holding the reins. So I thought, well, I'm in here. And the next minute I'm all tarted up and off we go to the ball. Well I was eyeing up the footman all night, I'm sure he was the one who came with the invitation, but not a chance. Prince Charming spotted me and decided I was the one and that was that. You can't say no to a prince.

He was mega-boring. An absolute woodentop on the dance floor. He took me out on the terrace. I thought oh no he's going to grope me. But he didn't. He knelt down on the cold flagstones and licked my feet. I knew it wasn't going to work for me, so I started to run. Too late. The clock chimed and my fate was sealed.

I couldn't get out of it you see. Not when the shoe fitted. There were government officials all over the place. It was marry him or the chop. No one had heard of women saying no. You did as you were told. I thought I'd got away from him. But for those bloody shoes. They weren't glass. They were plastic. See-thru plastic. I reckon she'd got them from some futuristic bargain basement. Sale item reduced. Though she said she made them herself. Someone told me she went on to become the Blue Peter muse. It was hell trying to run. When one fell off I ditched it in the lake and ran home in my bare feet. They fished it out of course.

So there I am, missus Charming. Another silly name. At least he let me keep my own clothes. I made this myself. Not just a pretty face you know, whatever the story-books say. Said he preferred me like this than in all that finery. He was quite kind. And I wouldn't have minded so much but for his foot fetish. Can't see the attraction myself. Chiropodists are the saints of humanity. Imagine picking over someone's ingrowing toenails. I think he was a bit disappointed. I mean yes I've got small feet but I also get terrible athlete's foot.

To start with I tried everything. Spent a fortune on ointments and poultices. My herbalist's bills nearly bankrupted the nation. Then I tried vinegar, which was a good deal cheaper, and it worked for a while, though I had to be careful applying it or it stripped the paint from my toenails. And he liked them ruby red. Said they reminded him of roses. He could be quite sweet sometimes. But toe-sucking wasn't my scene.

How to get out of it that was the question. I was getting desperate. Takes a spell to break a spell I thought and dashed off down to the kitchen and started cleaning the grate. I rubbed and wished and rubbed and wished and rubbed and wished and then the whole place began to shake and the floor started to tremble and disintegrate until there was a huge chasm between me and the fireplace and in the middle of this up comes the biggest most beautiful round table.

And around the table sit all these beautiful people all drinking from goblets and telling wonderful stories. And it's just like I've always known them. And I realise who they are. I mean I recognise them from pictures. There's Arthur with his sword and Sir Gawain (I knew who he was because of his green outfit) and all the rest of them. And of course Guinevere.

She's got it sussed has Guin. Has anyone she wants. I wonder if its her tits? Lovely stickyout tits she's got. Nipples like chapel hat pegs. I quite fancied her myself. But to be honest I wasn't in the mood for an affair. I just wanted to get back to my kitchen. So I think, well, I'll ask Guin for her advice. Some tips on how to get myself sorted. But every time I try to speak, the words come out distorted.

Guinevere / come over here / I said / let me know your secret, dear.
Cinders, you're a yummy chick / but the answer isn't quick, she says.
Watch the knights when they're at dinner / One of them will be a winner / Whoever finds beneath the table / the lock of hair that I plant / Gets to rump me on the rug / made of sweetest darkest sable.

A lock of hair plucked from your skull/ that's all?
Not from my head, that's far too dull, says Guin / the hair I give is full of honey / sweetened from within.

Now there's a thought / a pube / fresh caught / and softly curled beneath the wood/ where her next lover stood.

I watch them dine at night / See Lancelot smile with delight / see him stroke the lock of hair Guin has hidden by his chair.

Clever clever Guinivere / but why the need for someone else, I ask / for surely your King's s'posed to be first class? He might be technically a bastard / but he's really lasted / as a ruler with pizzazz. Everyone thinks he's the best.

He's quite a dish, says Guin, but surely one's entitled to alternatives. Besides, she whispers in my ear / Arthur is such a terrible farter. What's the problem with your prince?

Ah Guin, I'm not like you / fancying something bright and new / the point is I never wanted marriage / so adultery's not for me / I was just lusting for a man/ when I got a prince and carriage. Though I could take one of your knights/ to bed with me for a week of nights / I really want my kitchen back / to sit and scour the dirty pans / and dream of travelling distant lands / to be allowed to choose my life / maybe get together with someone / maybe just be a single housewife / who knows. I've tried a spell to break the spell / but it's not working very well.

You need help, says Guin / let's see / if we can get hold of Morgan le Fey.

So while the men go off to hunt, apart from Lancelot (who's got a stunt to pull upstairs with Guin) the women sit around the table drinking Arthur's gin.

The gossip flowed and wine / and tales / of how these women / rode the gales of life / to swim home safe / to Avalon. Some wore a knife / and others told / of how they'd won their knights of old / by riddles and by sorcery.

Tell me, I said conversationally, who is this Morgan le Fey? I'm waiting for an audience. And silence swept around the assembled company. One woman wept / another held her knuckles white upon the yellow wood / and several stood as if to go.

Please, I said / I need to know.

Morgan is both old and young / Descended from the great Morrigan / They say she appears as a raven / She's Arthur's sister, some believe... / And some that she's the womb in which he stirred.

So is she blessed with prophecy?
And all of them nod solemnly.
Morgan le Fey is Avalon/ says one with eyes of sapphire / she has the power to turn the very flowers into fire.

At last a bell rings from a room beyond the drafty hall / we all freeze / my name is called. Cucendron / Cucendron / come, listen to my song.

The women nudge me / go on / go on / don't prolong the agony.

A dark-haired vision dressed in silk sits in a room bathed in the milky light of the moon. This is no gipsy-rose-lee / but the one they call Morgan le Fey.
No crystal ball / nor cards nor all the trappings of the fairground here. Just long black curls / and the strangest eyes that ever on me did stare.

Cucendron / come here.

I took her hand / so pale and fair / I fell in love / that instant there. All long and slow she kissed my lips / and fleetingly caressed me.

Oh now I see a victim / a lost child of the sea / take this, she whispers softly / and presses close to me.

And I am swept upon a wave / of love / more swelling than the greatest of the ocean's. My heart leaps beating in my breast / I close my eyes / I take no breath / but let this seep right through my skin. And high above / in an indigo sky / the stars they burn / the moon does smile / and centuries pass by.

And gradually the world stopped spinning and I opened my eyes and she was gone. And where she'd stood upon the floor was this small beast *[indicates frog]*. And in the dust on the ground, were written these words:

If you believe in fairies
Including Morgan le Fey
Take me deep into the forest
Where a large pumpkin will be,
Kiss me thrice and make a wish
You'll no longer be a princess
You'll get back your heart's delight
At the seventh stroke of midnight.

So here I am. It must be nearly midnight. *[sits on pumpkin]* I wonder if this will turn into our transport.